Andreas Herteux

The Alternative Hegemony Model (AH Model)

The "invisible hand" of nurture for the better

© 2018 Andreas Herteux

Erich von Werner Society

Publisher: Erich von Werner Verlag
Translator : Astrid Vogel
ISBN: 978-3-9819-0061-3

Understand and Chance

The Erich von Werner Society assumes that the world is entering a new era.

These changes are because of or are accelerated by 5 factors, which in combination and interaction with each other will trigger a new era:

- Dealing with technological progress (e.g. digitization, biotechnology, human optimization)

- Rise of new competitors in world markets (e.g. Asian countries)

- Weakness of the Western world (e.g. instability, diminishing confidence in existing orders, loss of competitiveness, the political rise of China)

- Change of the environment (e.g. due to climate change, resource exploitation, environmental degradation)

- Overpopulation and missing life perspectives (e.g. due to the demographic development on the African continent)

These five factors are summarized by the Erich von Werner Society under the term **"Change of Times"**. This Change of Times, if not adequately countered, will completely change the global power relations, and seems to be for many people as a primary threat. It can be both a risk and an opportunity.

This Change of Times already has an extreme impact on the political, social and economic reality and its impact will get stronger.

For the western society, which represents a special field of research of the Erich von Werner Society, a complete transformation is to be expected. Little has remained of the classic realities of life and the age of individual collectivism of the past decades.In fact, society is shattered into many milieus and is slowly but surely drifting into an inevitable struggle of milieus in which individual realities of life stand against each other without any deeper understanding of each other.

How long and how intense this struggle of milieus will be not certain. What is certain is that society will enter the age of collective individualism in parallel. This uncertain course makes it necessary to find solutions to use the dynamic power of Change of Times for the benefit of humanity.

The aforementioned changes are already noticeable, because current political, social and economic developments, which are often perceived as divisive, corrosive and shocking, are ultimately the direct consequences of the Change of Times and will only intensify further.

They are the consequences of a global, interrelated phenomenon for which the explanatory patterns used so far are simply too simple and completely unfit. It is time to reject these obsolete interpretations and face the reality of change, because it is now the time to act before it is too late.

The storm won't wait, it is coming. One way to counter this storm ist the Alternative Hegemony Model (AH-Model).

Andreas Herteux

What is the fundamental idea behind the Alternative Hegemony Model (AH Model)?

The AH Model is an evolution of the current international political and economic system. It further develops the system, maintains existing structures and redirects negative dynamics.

The AH Model nurtures states and companies towards beneficial behaviour. This behaviour is rewarded and negative deviations are penalised. These incentives make positive behaviour both profitable and sustainable.

In doing so, the AH Model makes use of the same forces that are dominant in a capitalist system. However, it leads them in a new direction: the invisible hand of the market becomes the invisible hand of nurture.

This is achieved by bundling technological research and development work in newly established technology centres. These technology centres accumulate scientific competence, develop and test sustainable technologies for concrete use in member countries. Production and distribution are provided by co-operating companies, which continue to operate according to a market economy.

The AH Model is implemented and financed using an AH Fund. The AH Fund becomes the owner and market participant. It assumes the role of a sustainable super-company, which is managed by a management board in the same way as a joint-stock company is run. The AH Fund's Board of Directors is controlled by a body ("Supervisory Board") which is composed of representatives from the individual countries and which is obliged to render accountability to the national democratic authorities and at the donor conference. The developed technologies are only made available in the markets of those countries that demonstrate positive and sustainable behaviour ("minimum criteria"). Compliance with the criteria is also a prerequisite for participation in the AH Fund.

The aforementioned criteria (e.g. human rights, press freedom, social standards, etc.) are monitored continuously.

States that refuse to meet the criteria are excluded from technological progress, but are indirectly encouraged by the invisible hand of nurture to voluntarily adjust to the new system.

By preserving nation-states, retail management systems and cultural peculiarities it is to be expected that the populace will generally accept the change, and in turn it is rewarded for its positive and peaceful behaviour.

The financing is based on a percentage transfer of the gross social product. Further income is generated through licensing.

For a fee, the AH Fund awards usage and production licenses to companies that co-operate and comply with the criteria. The companies supply specified markets and are regulated for these products. In this way, sustainable technologies and progress are circulated using well-known distribution channels.

By means of the pure market power of the AH Fund, as well as the exclusivity it offers, existing companies will be encouraged to co-operate. This market power will also be used to procure resources (knowledge transfer, personnel, etc.).

The same applies to states and businesses: they will continue to be selfish and want to achieve maximum benefit for themselves. Nevertheless, positive behaviour is expected, i.e. cooperation and fulfilment of the criteria, profit maximisation and maximum benefits. For this reason, states and companies will largely adapt themselves voluntarily. The market forces are thus steered in a positive direction. The invisible hand of nurture has an effect and it is this which is the central element of the AH Model.

By using this beneficial behaviour and progress, the key problems of the planet can be solved or, at the very least, contained. In the long term, dictatorships and autocracies will become obsolete. A new world community will emerge taking cultural peculiarities into consideration while also looking to the future. An alternative hegemony that nurtures for the better.

What might the timetable for the AH Model look like?

Phase 0 (2019-2023)

- Dissemination of the AH Model idea

- Attempt starting up a grassroots movement

- Convince prominent advocates

- Lobby governments and businesses

- Establish the minimum criteria for states and enterprises

- Clarify the legal, economic and political dimension of the model

- Sustain a propaganda offensive

Phase 1 (2023-2025)

- First donor conferences

  o Participating countries must meet the minimum criteria

- o Autocracies and dictatorships are excluded
- o A step model should be possible for intermediate states

- Financing and control mechanisms as well as research and development goals should be defined

- Initial acquisition of personnel and knowledge

- First discussions with companies

- Conditions for the AH Fund

Phase 2 (2025-2030)

- AH Funds will set up the first technology centre

- Market power is used to initiate knowledge and personnel transfer

- Co-operation agreement with companies that meet or pursue the sustainability criteria (production conditions, environmental protection, etc.)

- Commencement of research and development work

Phase 3 (from 2030)

- The AH Fund becomes a capital-wielding market participant

- Research and production licensing to co-operating companies

- License only for beneficial states

- Monitoring licenses; possibly revoking them

- Stopping the technological transfer in case the minimum criteria are violated

- The nurture mechanism works ("the invisible hand of nurture")

Phase 4 (from 2033)

- New technologies cause a boom in the participating countries

- "Capitalist excesses" phase out

- The market economy remains the same

- The restrictions are only related to the licenses, but they impose beneficial entrepreneurial behaviour

- These states would become beacons of light and places of longing for the technologically underdeveloped entities

- The population of the "non-fulfillers" would perceive their backwardness

- Pressure is put on "non-fulfilling governments"

- Nation-states would therefore be trained into taking values and sustainability into account

- The invisible hand of nurture can cultivate a all-encompassing effect

Phase 5 (from 2063)

- Autocracies and dictatorships no longer exist

- Nation-states and cultural integrity are not questioned, but are driven in a positive direction by the incentive system. Thus, a high potential for identification is given

- Internationalism and patriotism are reconciled

- Research and development are no longer restricted by the idea of profit maximisation

- The AH Model will have solved major problems (e.g. climate issues, environmental protection, problems of democracy, and wars) and can now tackle further issues (e.g. overpopulation or global hunger)

Financing

- 2% of member states' GDP

- Alternative participation by the population, such as using the old-age pension system

- Alternative participation of sustainable enterprises is conceivable

- Income from licensing

- Revenue from purchased companies (e.g. through shares)

Abuse of power is controlled and prevented

The AH Fund is managed as a company and administered by a Board of Directors. The Board of Directors is accountable to the Supervisory Board, whose members are appointed by the donor countries. The Supervisory Board is accountable to the donor conference, the public and the national parliaments. Additionally, separate transparency requirements would also exist. An independent body would also be set up within the fund to monitor the minimum criteria for states and companies. The Board of Directors has no authority to issue directives to this body.

Feasibility

Realistic, since considerably profound co-operation has already been implemented in practical politics (e.g. the European Union, the World Bank, the International Monetary Fund) and considering that this suggestion is not a revolution, but rather an evolution for the benefit of the population - nurture for the better -

It is possible to conclude that:

The Alternative Hegemony Model is more than just a model of governance. This on its own would fail because of existing structures. Instead, it is all-inclusive and an idea. It introduces a new age. It preserves while also developing things further. Ultimately, the AH Model is the best invisible hand:

alternative hegemony through technology and nurture for the better.

Detailed consideration of the Alternative Hegemony Model (AH Model)

Fundamental and preliminary considerations

Our world is currently confronted by a multitude of problems and solving these would undoubtedly lead to a substantial improvement of general conditions. Some examples of this would be:

- Famines

- Climate change and natural disasters

- Diseases and epidemics

- Wars and political instability

- Poverty and economic imbalance

- Unknown consequences of technical developments

- Demographic trends

- Shift of global power

An eternal question is whether it makes sense to tackle these problems individually or whether it is better to find a global way forward: one system that automates the problems or, put succinctly, acts as a guiding, invisible hand which solves the problems and leads the world to a better future. Experiences from the past illustrate that attempts to solve an individually identified problem in an individual manner have almost always failed due to interrelationships; because, as a rule, it is only possible in a laboratory setting to separate problems such as climate change from other influences. It is for this reason that a global, all-encompassing approach is required.

However, the next problem arises from this idea. Practically all global approaches to solving these problems fail due to one banality: these approaches end up classifying the existing order as obsolete and inferior since they demand a revolution and major changes. Put more simply, most people are not dissatisfied with their existing way of life and culture. The same applies to politics and the economy. In short, they don't want to lose that which is habitual and which is a requirement for many global approaches. For this reason, the moment often comes when the populace tends to oppose too many changes. The current trends towards re-nationalisation, segregation of societies, loss of trust in established institutions and the so-called Establishment is a typical consequence of such attempts to carry out changes without the support of

17

the general populace. In addition to this, there are of course other interest groups. In most cases one only thinks of the conflict between economic expansion and climate protection.

However, it is necessary to use a model that incorporates the currently existing order, its strengths and dynamics, but which guides it in a direction that will be to the benefit of all. To create such a model is ambitious, but necessary, since the changes would not be accepted otherwise and would end up facing massive resistance.

The Alternative Hegemony Model (AH Model) is a holistic approach. It is ultimately the continued development - an evolution - of the existing order.

Consequently, this is not a matter of tackling a single problem, to reform or develop a system of government. Instead, the aim is to adopt an entirely new approach that could resolve all dimensions, from the form of government to social issues, from the economy to technological development, from education to identification and which also involves all the relevant interest groups.

This paper will therefore not only address corrections to existing systems, but also proposes a realistic and feasible solution to resolve or mitigate many of the most pressing problems humanity faces today.

The AH Model rewards positive behaviour and punishes negative behaviour. It is a model that is designed to nurture states, businesses and people into meeting and fulfilling established norms. Furthermore, the AH Model is not based on morality. It is instead based on egotism and the drive to maximize profit. It is dependent on *homo economicus*. However, it transforms the world so that this maximisation will only succeed with sustainable, positive behaviour. In brief: an invisible hand uses natural dynamics and nurtures for the better, i.e. an alternative hegemony.

A description of what such a system could look like is presented in more detail below.

It should, however, be noted in advance that such a complex system contains a great number of detailed issues which cannot be discussed in depth in the limited and predetermined framework of this paper, thus these issues are often only implied.

In some areas there is also no deliberate definition: the AH Model is not rigid, but flexible and pragmatic. Therefore, there are often several viable ways to conceivably achieve the required goals, meaning that a dogmatic definition would, in many cases, be of little use.

The Alternative Hegemony Model is feasible and implementation could begin immediately, turning the skills of the world towards a better future.

The Alternative Hegemony Model (AH Model)

What is the AH Model?

The AH Model (Alternative Hegemony Model) is an evolution of the current international political and economic system. It further develops the system, maintains existing structures and redirects negative dynamics.

The AH Model nurtures states, companies and even people towards sustainable behaviour. This behaviour is rewarded and negative deviations are penalised. As a result of these incentives, positive behaviour becomes profitable, sustainable and will be striven towards out of pure egotism.

In doing so, the AH Model makes use of the same forces that are dominant in a capitalist system. However, it guides them in a new direction: the invisible hand of the market becomes the invisible hand of nurture for the better.

The AH Model makes positive behaviour worthwhile, since it promises profit maximisation for all parties involved. As a result, sustainable actions are accepted and even preferred.

The fundamental idea

Many ideas and concepts are conceptualised from an idealistic point of view and in order for them to work, mankind must in principle be good. However, the AH Model starts out from the assumption that states, businesses and people are mostly egotistical and strive to achieve maximum benefits.

Consequently, the model does not convert, but rather uses the natural urge and redirects it. With the help of the model, positive and sustainable behaviour leads to profit maximisation. Thus, states, corporations and people will behave positively or adapt their behaviour to fit the model for purely egotistic reasons. Furthermore, the AH Model works without uprooting ways of identification, system changes in the individual countries, or incisions into normal, everyday existence.

Basically, the AH Model completes capitalism and simultaneously reconciles it with social ideals by transforming a selfish attitude towards betterment.

Core component of the AH Model: alternative hegemony through technology

The core component of the AH Model is technology. Through it, the system unfolds its power and achieves an alternative hegemony over the course of many decades. This is achieved by bundling technological research and development work in newly established technology centres. These centres combine scientific expertise and develop and test sustainable technologies. Its size, financial resources and prestige will establish the largest research and development departments in the world and will thus become the dominant factor for a moral hegemony through technology and nurturace for the better.

Where should we begin?

In addition to a comprehensive public campaign and theoretical preparatory work, the donor conference represents the beginning, where countries participating in the AH Model will agree on principle issues such as:

- How will the budget be used?

- What will be researched?

- Which legal and economic conditions must be created?

- How will the AH Fund be shaped exactly?

Since the donor conference also exercises a control function, it will reconvene at periodic intervals.

Who will participate in the technology centres or in the donor conference?

The technology centres will be operated with an AH Fund, which is determined by the donor conference. This variant is nothing new and has already been successfully tested with the International Monetary Fund (IMF). Only countries that meet the established minimum criteria will be able to deposit in the AH Fund. Characteristic criteria may include:

- Evaluation of democratic structures

- Compliance with human rights

- Freedom of the press

- Social standards

In general, all necessary indicators already exist. They would only need to be fixed and monitored in a catalogue.

More information regarding the criteria for participating countries

Compliance with the minimum criteria is relevant to the participation of a country in the AH Fund. Put in concrete terms, these could look as follows:

- Evaluation of democratic structures

    A range of different methods are already used by NGOs, government bodies and business agencies. The Democracy Index of "The Economist" has, for example, a very broad scope. According to this index, 19 states can be classified as complete and another 56 as incomplete democracies.

    However, the above index is only one example of many attempts at such a measurement. Irrespective of which type is finally preferred, the means and procedures already exist. On this point it would only be necessary to reach an agreement

- Compliance with human rights

    As in the case of democratic structures, there are already numerous measuring methods and statistics that attempt an objective assessment.

- Freedom of the press and of expression

Here, too, an analogy exists; since ultimately, a country with limited freedom of the press and freedom of expression will always contain a potential for conflict, which could in the end even be directed against positive structures. For this reason, it is necessary to aspire to maximum freedom. Again, methods for measuring already exist.

- <u>Social standards</u>

  A difficult point is comparing social standards, since different economies and mentalities interact at this point. It would be desirable for a citizen of a country to be able to access adequate resources in the event of illness, poverty, unemployment or old age. However, it must be noted that such demands are not borne by all in democracies. On the other hand, the criteria listed here are only suggestions. In the case of social standards, a small common denominator could therefore be established at the beginning, which could then be sustainably extended over the years.

- <u>Level of education</u>

  Since education is ultimately subject to the sovereignty of the respective state, fundamental comparability is possible.

However, it would be necessary to take different training systems into account. Since educational systems often lead to ideological trench battles, evaluation criteria should be based on basic questions, such as the following:

a) Do equal opportunities exist regardless of background?

b) Are starting disadvantages compensated?

c) Is the education system freely accessible to everyone and in all its forms?

d) Is it expansive?

e) Is the education system capable of conveying education in such a way that the implementation of the qualification can lead to a profession which assures the person's own livelihood?

This is certainly not an exhaustive list, especially since measurement methods already exist that penetrate much more deeply into the matter.

The only relevant aspect is that an objective and no ideological consideration is made of the education system; cultural, mostly national, peculiarities should be intensively examined but no fixed quotas should be used for the assessment.

- Other criteria, such as arms exports, climate and environmental legislation, consumer rights, corruption or lobbying can also be considered

Overall, useful procedures and recording methods already exist. It is therefore only necessary to adapt and concentrate them, something that an expert commission could create in a matter of a few weeks.

At the end of the day, the smallest denominator will certainly be the starting point, but this is still so great that autocracies and dictatorships will not have a chance to become partners in the model.

Where do the financial resources for funding the technology centres come from?

They come from the member states that finance an AH Fund, which in turn manages the technology centres. It is suggested that per year, 2% of the GDP of the respective country would be provided, which should supply the AH Fund with sufficient capital.

Once the technology centres have been established, the research and development results would be used to award licenses and generate revenues.

Later, it may be an interesting option to re-structure the pension systems of the member countries so that the original contributions also flow into the AH Fund which then also pays out the pensions. But that is a dream for the future.

Where does the technology centre get the knowledge and the staff?

The AH Fund is endowed with 2% of each country's GDP. This corresponds to an annual sum of approx. 720 billion US Dollars and creates a market power which should make the acquisitions, purchases and transfer of knowledge easy, even if a complete takeover is necessary. We also recommend a propaganda campaign that highlights the prestige of the role.

Thus, the AH Fund would use its market position to:

- Recruit qualified personnel from existing companies

- Attract new talent at the universities

- Possibly to buy up shares in whole companies and to take over their research and development departments

- To enter into cooperative ventures with companies that make their R&D department available in order to subsequently benefit from the licenses as long as these companies meet the set sustainability criteria

Why should a state participate in the AH Model or an AH Fund in the first place?

It can be assumed that potential member states will initially come from the western hemisphere, since the majority of the impulses (e.g. European Union, Nato, UN) have originated from this geographical area. It is precisely this western world, however, which is currently facing extreme problems:

- <u>Loss of competitiveness to non-democratic orders</u>

  This can be seen in the current indices, which indicate that the western, mostly democratic, world has clearly lost its competitiveness and location advantages. A relevant study for this would be, for example, one from the

IMD (World Competitiveness Center), in which this thesis is demonstrated.

The assumption that the Asian states will overtake the West is no longer a question of the "whether", but rather only a matter of "when".

A weakening economy will always have an effect on stability and the society, and portends the beginning of disorder and chaos.

- <u>Threatened failure of international alliances and treaties (e.g. EU)</u>

In addition to the loss of competitiveness, more and more projects are failing to vitalize and strengthen their own position.

The European Union does not appear to be in a position to form a single economic area. Indirect transfer payments and long-term crises have been the consequences, of which "Brexit" is only a negative climax. Although it will be possible to support the construct for many years, competitiveness will again suffer as a result of this support. To sum it up, the EU is in a deadlock and requires thorough and comprehensive reforms.

The large transatlantic free trade agreement, which wanted nothing less than to shield a newer, much larger market, has failed when considering the present state of affairs.

- Loss of confidence in established institutions and segregation of the population; re-nationalisation

In the Western world the phenomenon of re-nationalisation is increasingly a factor. In part, societies are divided and even medial whitewashing cannot transfigure the real situation. In many Western societies, just one catalyst would suffice to unhinge the existing order. It was possible to observe this twice in the past year (Brexit, Donald Trump). Meanwhile, one can expect that a considerable part of the population is skeptical about the prevailing system and, if necessary, is merely waiting for alternatives to choose from. It is a dangerous and widely underestimated situation which has ultimately been caused by bad politics.

- Partial demographic problems

According to current studies, there are more people over the age of 65 in the European Union than under the age of 15. This means nothing less than that the societies are ageing drastically and this will have an extreme impact on the society and economy.

It is precisely the systems in which pensions are financed through a pay-as-you-go system that are facing a demographic catastrophe and that will be compelled to find solutions to this problem in the very near future.

- Sluggishness, too little migration, undermining and influences on democratic processes

Another problem is the erosion of democratic entities due to encrustations, power concentration, the market power of the established forces, lobbying and the submission to supranational entities. On the one hand, the influence of the ordinary citizen appears to be too small, on the other hand, the alternative factors of influence are too great. For this reason, the democratic structures are in need of complete reconsideration and reworking.

- Social issues, infrastructure and identification problems, dwindling educational services

In addition to those factors already mentioned, a variety of other factors also play a role. However, to address each of these in detail would exceed the scope of this short presentation.

All in all, the tendency is undoubtedly toward the Western world irrevocably losing its supremacy over the course of the coming decades. It is therefore being forced to reform and such attempts, whether they are free trade agreements or a consolidation of the European Union, are always based on the idea of retaining one's own position and preparing for a competition, even if this is not communicated at the level of intensity that might be necessary.

Some of these attempts have been successful (e.g. Nato, UN) some have already failed (e.g. the Transatlantic Free Trade Agreement), others are still operating, but they lack acceptance (e.g. European Union).

Thus, there is a willingness to co-operate in international projects, including those requiring a high level of investment.

On the one hand we have this willingness to co-operate, on the other we have the unalterable necessity of retaining one's own prosperity. These factors are what make the AH Model viable.

However, this does not mean that the door is open only to the Western world. The AH Model welcomes any state that meets the minimum criteria.

What would be researched?

The research itself is manifold. However, the prerequisite is sustainability and use for improvement. Regarding this point, an agreement must be reached at donor conferences. Topics may include:

- Increasing efficiency in the use of renewable energies (e.g. increasing the capacity of batteries in electric vehicles)

- Development of seeds for cultivation areas with difficult climates

- Basic medical research for diseases, to generate patents

- Further development of digital transmission channels (e.g. more efficient networks and setting up standards)

- Other topics

What is the nature of this AH Fund and how is it controlled?

The AH Fund becomes the owner and market participant. It assumes the role of a sustainable super-company. The AH Fund is managed as a company and administered by a Board of Directors.

The Board of Directors is accountable to the Supervisory Board, whose members are appointed by the donor countries. The Supervisory Board is accountable to the donor conference, the public and the national parliaments. Additionally, separate transparency requirements would also exist. An independent body would also be set up within the fund to monitor the minimum criteria for states and companies. The Board of Directors has no authority to issue directives to this body.

In principle, it is possible to make a comparison to the International Monetary Fund (IMF), which illustrates that such an idea such as this can effectively be put into practice, even if the content-related objective is actually different. It is not necessary to reinvent the much-lauded wheel; instead, existing experience can be used.

What is the relationship of the AH Fund to the companies?

As the largest market participant, the AH Funds has market power which it can also use. It has the possibility of buying up companies and is able to compete or co-operate with them. The company grants usage and production licenses only to those companies that meet the sustainability criteria (e.g. wages, social standards, working conditions, etc.). At the same time, licenses are also used to determine the countries in which a product may be sold. As a result, similar to the outcome among the states, the fund forces companies to adapt and become sustainable. Thus, the nightmare of the world economy being governed by large corporations could be terminated prematurely. In exceptional cases, it is also conceivable that individual companies could integrate their research and development departments into the AH Fund. However, this should only be allowed after completing very severe sustainability tests.

What criteria does the AH Fund apply to companies?

As with states, the fund co-operates only with those companies that display sustainable behaviour. The criteria for this would be:

- Transparency

Any company seeking a license shall have specific transparency obligations, which primarily concern the use of those licenses. In this way, it should be possible to ensure sustainable use

- Market restrictions

  Since the research and development work is only intended to benefit sustainable states, the licensees are required to specify the sales markets for products with a license and these markets are restricted to the participating countries. Other products are not affected.

- Production conditions

  Sustainability also includes the production conditions for all of the company's products. Degrading conditions will be sanctioned with direct action which culminates in the license being revoked.

- Environmental protection

  Companies that repeatedly fail to comply with environmental regulations shall only be granted licenses once they have proven to have eliminated these deficiencies. The same applies if these violations occur at a later date

- <u>Interdependency of states or other enterprises</u>

  Companies must be examined to determine whether states or other companies that do not meet the AH Model's standard have an influence and it may be necessary to reject them.

- <u>Treatment of Employees</u>

  A further noteworthy point is how they treat their own employees. Interesting questions would include:

  - Is the remuneration adequate?

  - Is the remuneration fair?

  - What is the history of downsizing?

  - What is the situation with temporary employment?

  - Does an occupational pension scheme exist?

  - What are the opportunities for advancement?

  - Is corporate co-determination possible?

o What is the relationship with the unions?

As with the states, there are also a variety of criteria that can be used today to decide whether the respective consortium is suitable for licensing or investment.

On the whole, the AH Model not only forces companies to introduce transparency, but also encourages sustainable behaviour, since any violation leads to licenses being revoked. Nevertheless, this enforcement is not direct, but simply the pressure of the market. In the end, the companies will not accept the new system for reasons of sustainability, but simply because this path is the one that leads to maximum profit. Exclusion from the licenses would bring economic disadvantages. The invisible hand of nurture also works here.

Are sustainable companies entitled to obtain licenses?

If companies meet the minimum criteria, they must obtain a legal claim for a licensing procedure.

However, this does not alter the fact that the licenses involve restrictions on use (production and sales areas).

Would it be possible for front companies to be used to gain access to the technology?

The idea that a state or a group of companies that do not fulfil the minimum criteria are able to buy up or buy into a "clean" company through numerous detours would be possible, but would ultimately fail due to the transparency or disclosure obligations which are imposed on the company.

Is it really possible to prevent products that are based on licenses from also being sold in critical markets?

Sales in undesirable markets can of course be legally prohibited and sanctioned. Such embargoes already exist today. One example is the weapons trade. It is also important to consider whether it is necessary to exclude every product from all undesirable markets. The decision in each case should depend on the product.

Nonetheless, the illegal path will never be fully shut down, but such deviations are not really relevant to the AH Model.

Why should the AH Fund be more successful in research and development than free companies are?

Firstly, the AH Fund is managed as a company, albeit with special transparency requirements. However, it also has access to greater financial resources, more centralised knowledge, and is not fettered by research in terms of profit maximisation. In short:

Using its market power, image and will it will succeed in acquiring the best of the best for a good cause and with highest commitment.

Does the AH Model replace capitalism?

No, it only directs the forces of capitalism onto a better path. The intention is not to abolish the free market. Every company is free to ignore the fund and act as it has to date. The AH Fund is ultimately only the largest market participant, which sets conditions for business that are associated with it. The market will remain and act as it has. Purely as a result of the AH Fund's market power, the market will be steered towards sustainability by the invisible hand of nurture and this without needing to use planned economies.

For a fee, the AH Fund awards usage and production licenses to companies that co-operate and comply with the criteria. The companies supply specified markets and are regulated for these products. In this way, sustainable technologies and progress are circulated using well-known distribution channels.

This approach does not stop the free market because it is up to the companies to decide what products they will create and at what quality. On the contrary, competition would even be promoted.

What about states that have not yet met the minimum criteria despite all efforts?

States that are on the road to meeting the minimum criteria can be involved in a step-by-step approach ("Candidates"). In this case a similar structure to States joining the European Union could be used.

What happens to states that do not want to meet the minimum criteria?

The developed technologies are only made available in the markets of those countries that demonstrate positive and sustainable behaviour ("minimum criteria").

The aforementioned criteria (e.g. human rights, press freedom, social standards, etc.) are monitored continuously by an independent supervisory board.

States that refuse to meet the criteria are excluded from technological progress, but are indirectly forced by the invisible hand of nurture to voluntarily adjust to the new system. So, just as they cannot escape the power of the market today, they will not be able to escape the power of nurture in the future. Dictatorships and autocracies will become obsolete.

What about the counterproductive nation-states that have already achieved a high level of technology?

Undoubtedly successful autocracies and authoritarian structures do exist. In these cases, the invisible hand of education will not work immediately or may require a longer preparation time. It is also possible that serious conflicts may occur.

However, these conflicts would be completely independent of the AH Model. Since the West does not want to abandon its pre-eminence without a fight, conflicts are actually inevitable. It would therefore be naive to believe that the AH Model generates conflicts. On the contrary, dividing lines would only become more clearly visible and would finally be overcome.

And what about the people?

The previous sections have focused primarily on the behaviour of states and enterprises as well as on the economic system in general. However, every evolution ultimately affects the citizen in their own country and for them the AH system changes life for the better:

- Considering that states have to fulfil the minimum criteria, such as a democratic order, the observance of human rights and equality before the law, these criteria will become irrevocably cemented into place

- On the other hand, the companies are also nurtured into being sustainable. Environmental degradation, exploitation or wage dumping will phase out

- The economy will flourish as a result of the new technologies. Jobs will be created and general prosperity would become the norm

- New technologies, e.g. in medical engineering would improve the life of the individual

- The AH system guarantees cultural integrity, meaning that the people lose nothing and keep on gaining

- etc.

In total, the individual is the big winner of the AH system. It would indeed work without the citizens, but this is not considered to be meaningful, since exclusion or even an authoritarian coercion in a model that wants to improve the lives of all is neither necessary nor expedient.

Will the often split societies accept the AH Model?

According to current studies, confidence in the established institutions of the Western world has declined significantly. Some societies are even considered to be divided.

The AH Model does not contribute to this widening gap, but instead reconciles. Many forces that are incompatible with one another in the current political system will be brought together. Some examples of this include:

- Internationalism vs nationalism

The AH Model affects the lives of all directly or indirectly and improves them in the long term.

Nevertheless, it simultaneously never intervenes in cultural identity. Thus, a compromise has been found for both sides.

- Free market vs welfare state

The AH Model uses the forces of the free market and redirects them. This makes sustainable behaviour worthwhile and promises a profit to the majority. This sustainability will cause an economic upswing and thus also opportunities to create a suitable welfare state. At the same time, however, the AH Model does not engage in the free market. No entrepreneur has to fear expropriation.

- Parliamentary vs direct democracy

The AH Model sets minimum criteria. How these are met is not of interest. The precise structure of the basic democratic order is the responsibility of the countries and depends on their democratic traditions.

How can broad support be obtained from the outset?

Before the AH Model can be introduced, it is necessary to spread the idea itself. In principle, two routes for enforcement are conceivable, both of which should be pursued in parallel:

- Bottom-up

    o Spreading the idea on the Internet

    o actively approaching democratic institutions

    o Starting petitions

    o Creating a grassroots movement

    o Starting a movement for a better future

- Top-down

    o Propagating the idea using celebrities and the media

    o Convincing relevant organisations and politicians of the AH Model's benefits

In total, the AH Model has the potential to be both: an idea which is supported by the people and also one that can be brought to humanity.

What does the timetable for the AH Model for a better world look like?

Phase 0 (2019-2023)

In the preparatory phase, it would be important to present the AH Model to the general public and to communicate, above all, in clear and simple terms, that it is not a further attempt to unhinge the word. Rather, it is a system which preserves cultural peculiarities and traditions while only guiding those forces which often seem to be out of control onto a better path. It is also appropriate at this early stage to woo prominent supporters and actively engage in lobbying in the legislative and executive branches.

Ultimately, both a grassroots movement and support from the establishment should be accomplished.

At the same time, it would be important to actively promote the model in schools, universities and specialists during this phase, in order to ensure the procurement of personnel and to be able to begin initial discussions with companies.

Simultaneously, a catalogue will be drawn up specifying the minimum criteria which must be adhered to in order to participate in the AH Model.

Typical criteria would be respect for human rights, press freedom or the existence of a democratic system. The existing bodies of the UN and research studies can be used for this purpose. For states that do not meet the criteria, a step by step system would be developed with which the norm could be reached gradually.

In general, all legal, economic and theoretical foundations should be fixed in such a way that ultimately only giving the green light would be necessary.

Phase 1 (2023-2025)

The initial donor conferences will take place during the first phase. In these, the budget, framework conditions and technologies to be developed would be defined. Similarly, the ways in which personnel and knowledge will be acquired should be put in concrete terms and implementation initiated.

Decisions on the management of the AH Fund shall be finalised.

In short: the theory, which will have been prepared for many years, will be applied practically following concrete decisions.

In parallel to these processes, final talks with companies will take place to explore future co-operation and licensing agreements. The minimum criteria will be articulated and must be fulfilled within a given time frame.

The AH Fund will be launched jointly when the participating countries deposit 2% of their gross domestic product. This would correspond to a yearly payment of 720 billion US dollars if only the European Union and the USA were to participate. The mechanism for monitoring the criteria will also installed.

In principle, it can be assumed that the preparation will take several years and the AH Fund will only be able to start in 2025.

Phase 2 (2025-2030)

In the second phase, public communication should be intensified. General approval would need to be achieved.

The AH Fund would at this point have the means to build the first technology centre.

For the start, 3 years have been estimated for the construction. During this time, professional staff would be recruited. This should work without any problems due to targeted advertisement at the universities and suitably high pay, and by simultaneously generating a positive image.

The transfer of knowledge appears to be more difficult, but the supreme market power should also be used consistently. Corporations may be bought up or brought into the fold, to the extent that they are already state owned. Companies whose research and development departments are not included will subsequently be excluded from production or license agreements. Basically, there are many efficient ways to transfer knowledge.

Following the construction of the first technology centre, research and development work may begin, with initial results expected in 2030.

Phase 3 (from 2030)

In this way, the AH Fund will become the largest research and development institution in the world and probably the only one that is under democratic control. At this point, it would be able to award licenses for products and patents to companies that can demonstrate their ability to adapt. These will then develop, produce, market and sell the products. However, only in those countries that meet the minimum criteria of the AH Model. These criteria are continually checked by the UN and if necessary the licenses are revoked.

In principle, it would also be worth considering whether the AH Fund could perhaps subsidise products or production facilities in certain regions. Nevertheless, we advise against this because the AH Model does not wish to interfere with national autonomy or the free market.

Both companies and states will be aware that the path to new technologies will be curtailed in the event of negative behaviour and so they will turn towards the good even if it is partially for selfish reasons.

Thus, for the first time, the invisible hand of nurture will affect states, enterprises and indirectly even the people. Wars would become unproductive. The technologies and resulting products will resolve the primary problems

Phase 4 (from 2033)

The new technologies will create an economic boom and the digital turning point will have been achieved, simply because the free market will have been essentially preserved and the integrity of the participating countries is not affected, apart from the nurturing aspect. Cultural diversity is not attacked by the AH Model.

Through economic prosperity and progress, "good" states will again becoming beacons of light and places of longing for technologically backward entities. The population in autocracies and dictatorships will be lagging behind and governments would be forced to change. The same applies to companies that will not yet have achieved the criteria. The invisible hand of nurture exerts pressure. This pressure would be mediated by shareholders or by the populace, who would demand reform or even topple authoritarian regimes. In this way, all nation-states would gradually be nurtured into taking values and sustainability into account. The same applies to companies that would have significant disadvantages in terms of competition if they refuse to change their behaviour.

These uniform standards make it even easier for the world to come closer together. The invisible hand of nurture can cultivate a all-encompassing effect

Phase 5 (from 2060)

Autocracies and dictatorships no longer exist. It is self-evident that the AH Fund controls the research and development of the planet.

Since the nation-states were never questioned, but were instead driven in a positive direction through the incentive system, the potential for identification is high.

The technological developments of the AH Model will have solved major problems (e.g. climate issues, environmental protection, problems of democracy, and wars) and can now tackle further issues (e.g. overpopulation or global hunger) An alternative hegemony has been established.

The AH Model has made the world a better place.

Summary

The Alternative Hegemony Model is more than just a model of governance. This on its own would fail because of existing structures. It is all-inclusive. It introduces a new age. It preserves while also developing things further.

It is self-evident that many details would still have to be clarified with such a comprehensive idea. However, it is designed to ensure that pragmatism and flexibility will prevail instead of dogmatics.

Of course, the time plan established here is also ambitious, but it seems more sensible to have a tighter agenda than a permanent non-binding process. In the end, the serious problems cannot be postponed.

There is still time for the world to effect a transition in full strength towards the good or, at the very least, for the better. However, this could change with every day we delay. Consequently, now is the time to take a step into the future, not to wait until the possibilities for action have been restricted to the extent where action is no longer possible and at best only a reaction could be effected. A system currently exists, however it does not seem to be able to solve existing problems in a way that keeps the good of all in mind.

Markets alone will not make the world a better place. Neither will the belief in ideologies or utopias. As strongly as the latter are propagated by minorities and fanatics, they will never find acceptance among the masses, and in the end only provoke divisions and hatred.

In the end, there is only one solution: an alternative hegemony established with technology and which uses nurture to bring about improvement in order to avoid resistance. Or put simply: the AH Model.

The model of alternative hegemony as a problem solver

The alternative hegemony model is more than a theoretical construct. It is an idea. A spark that can cause a wildfire. It is the notion that it is not yet too late to lead the world in a positive direction.

Such ideas are always ambitious and have often failed in the course of history or have involved horrifying consequences. However, what is the reality? Those states which are trying to represent ideal values are becoming weaker and are losing their competitive advantages. Autocracies are now also economically successful. Attempts to restore the old supremacy are failing or find little acceptance. However, history does not wait. The current trend will continue: segregated societies, loss of international influence and a competition that illustrates that at least economic success can work without the hassle of things like human rights or democracy.

This means no less than that the possibilities for changes that are still present will begin to fade in a few years time. For this reason, it is time to start now, before the protagonists are overtopped and turned into extras.

Improvement always involves honesty and an admission to one's self. The honesty to admit that the previous order is shifting and the admission that many counter-measures threaten to fail.

The time to improve partly failed experiments or to conceptualise isolated solutions, the practical implementation of which ultimately fails due to lobbying or fears, is over.

It is time to hit a home run. It is an idea that can be put into practice quickly and effectively, that does not require uprooting the identity of the masses, and that does not misunderstand the nature of mankind, which is not solely characterised by love and altruism. It is an idea which promises to inspire and yet also offers individual benefit. The AH Model is such an idea. The egotistic turn towards good.

It is self-evident that such a model is difficult to illustrate in just a few words. Nevertheless, this has been achieved in this paper and will still be developed further a bit.

How will the AH Model secure basic values?

Compliance with fundamental rights and values is one of the conditions to be able to benefit from the AH Model in the first place.

The AH Model uses existing dynamics to nurture for the better. Similar to the invisible hand of the market, there is an invisible hand of nurture. Not only does it safeguard basic values, it also allows them to be implemented for the first time in many countries. Positive behaviour is rewarded; negative behaviour is sanctioned.

Thus, observing basic values becomes profitable and desirable, over and above any moral considerations.

This will be illustrated by two examples:

- Right to freedom of expression

  Freedom of expression is a higher good. Countries where freedom of expression is suppressed will not be given the opportunity to participate in the AH Fund. These countries will not be able to obtain any licenses, they will also not benefit from the profits, and even sales of the products would be restricted on their markets. In this way, they are cut off from the future. This process puts indirect pressure on the governments, which may also be intensified directly by the citizens.

  As a result of this pressure, freedom of expression could be enforced for the first time in many countries. On the other hand, it is also profitable for the government, since the new rights do not necessarily have to be directed against them. These rights could enable a new era of prosperity, which could possibly also be associated with the current regime.

It is irrelevant whether ultimately the government is toppled or adapts, the invisible hand of nurture has an effect.

- Conditions of social production

The AH Fund only co-operates with companies that meet sustainability criteria and social standards. Any company that manufactures its products under bad conditions is excluded from the licensing. The company now has two options: it can either renounce the licenses or improve the conditions. Considering that a renunciation of the co-operation would lead to competitive disadvantages in the long term, adjustment is preferred. This choice is made simply because this solution promises maximum profits.

This naturally also affects the working conditions of the employees. If these are improved, workers will be given a better and more worthy life. In this way, the invisible hand of nurture indirectly contributes to improving the personal situation of many and thus enforces basic values.

Decision-making competence and efficiency of decision-making processes

The decision-making competencies established in the AH Model depend on the respective phase. During the implementation phase, it will be necessary to define the framework conditions of the fund and agree on objectives and criteria.

Once the AH Fund has been launched, these donor conferences continue their existence and continue to specify the areas of focus. The fund itself is managed by a board of directors and is essentially managed as a company. However, extended transparency requirements exist internally and externally. Within the fund, the supervisory body should also be permanently responsible for monitoring the criteria. Nevertheless, external solutions could also be conceivable in this regard. However, the supervisory body in charge of the minimum criteria is not a recipient of orders from the Board of Directors and should be independent.

The Board of Directors is controlled by a Supervisory Board composed of representatives of the national parliaments. This implies an analogy to a stock corporation. The Supervisory Board is accountable to the national parliaments, the donor conference and the public, and votes on major decisions.

These budgeting processes are passed on to the AH Fund's Board of Directors and normal business processes follow.

All in all, the AH Fund is an organisation which is managed in the same rigorous manner as a company. The Board of Directors receives targets and a budget, but then has no more restrictions for achieving them.

Thus, decision-making processes and efficiency are guaranteed.

Effective resolution of urgent problems

The AH Model is an all-encompassing approach that can lead the existing political and economic system into a new and better future. It is a new idea, which has emerged from a historical configuration and which can be presented in such a way as to find supporters. For this reason, the AH Model is capable of solving urgent problems such as:

- Violations of human rights

   The AH Model rigorously sanctions violations of human rights with nonacceptance, license revocation and by withholding products. On the other hand, compliant behaviour is rewarded.

- Dictatorships and autocracies

As in the case of human rights, dictatorships and autocracies will be forced by the hand of nurture to open up their societies or they will have to live with revolts and uprisings among their population which will become disconnected from technological advancements.

- Excesses of capitalism

Since the AH Fund is a powerful market participant it would be able to set standards. Lasting resistance would lead to demise. Thus, companies will adapt and will keep sustainability in mind. Not for the benefit of mankind, but for self-interest, which in this case actually produces something good.

- Epidemics and diseases

Combining research capacities makes it easier to combat diseases and epidemics. In addition, the AH Fund neither retains any knowledge as a result of economic considerations nor does it prevent development.

- Environmental protection and ecological disasters

  One of the main research areas would be sustainable technology. Here too, a reference is made to the utmost importance of pooling and an approach which is not based on profit maximisation. In addition, the AH Model would indirectly educate towards environmental protection.

- Wars and the use of weapons of mass destruction

  Wars and the use of weapons of mass destruction would result in an exclusion from the fund, as well as sanctions on licenses and products.

  Additionally, the effect of the invisible hand of nurture could lead to the development of and investment in such weapons becoming unproductive.

- Climate change, famine and population explosion

  The consequences of climate change, such as the desertification of areas for cultivation, can be overcome by research. Hunger is eliminated and the country's prosperity increases. As prosperity increases, the birth rates generally fall

- Artificial intelligence

  Since AI would be researched and developed centrally and without financial interests, it is possible to hope that it will not be used abusively or in a degenerative manner.

- etc.

Resources and financing

Funding is initially achieved by the member states that would annually contribute 2% of their GDP to the AH Fund and would adopt a budget. This would provide the AH Fund with sufficient financial resources. With the GDP of the US and EU, the cumulative annual sum for support would still amount to approx. 720 billion dollars per year.

Once the technology centres have been established, the research and development results would be used to award licenses and generate revenues. Seriously estimating the income from licensing is unnecessary, but it is possible to assume that the technology centres could be economically viable after only a few years.

Later, it may be an interesting option to re-structure the pension systems of the member countries so that the original contributions also flow into the AH Fund which then also pays out the pensions. Nevertheless, this is an idea for the future which could firstly increase the acceptance of the model and secondly provides a way for the citizens to participate in the fund.

As a result of the capitalisation, the AH Fund would have access to substantial financial resources. With these funds, it would be easy to acquire the necessary knowledge on the market and to pay a maximum price for it. At the same time, it is advisable to advertise at universities at an early stage.

It would also be conceivable to simply buy up stock market shares and to separate entire Research and Development departments to merge them with the technology centre. We strive to offer a comparative figure: during the period when the fund would receive about 720 billion annually, the value of the most expensive company in the world can be estimated to around 590 billion (as of 2016).

Consequently, the AH Fund's market power should be so great that nothing would be able to resist it.

Feasibility

The implementation of the AH Model is far less complex than the establishment of the European Union, the UN or NATO. Nevertheless, all three of these institutions have been implemented. They prove that even more intensive co-operation is not excluded by the individual states.

It goes without saying, however, that every idea needs supporters who are also interested in its fulfilment, otherwise it would never grow beyond the theoretical aspect. The same is true for the AH Model. In principle, two ways of enforcement are conceivable:

• bottom-up

  • Disseminating the idea on the Internet

  • Actively approaching democratic institutions

  • Starting petitions

  • Creating a grassroots movement

  • Starting a movement for a better future

• Top-down

- Propagating the idea using celebrities and the media

- Convincing relevant organisations and politicians of the AH Model's benefits

In total, the AH Model has the potential to be both: an idea which is supported by the people and also one that can be brought to humanity. In principle, the individual in the AH system is definitely not a loser:

- Considering that states have to fulfil the minimum criteria, such as a democratic order, the observance of human rights and equality before the law, these criteria will become irrevocably cemented into place

- On the other hand, the companies are also nurtured into being sustainable. Environmental degradation, exploitation or wage dumping will phase out

- The economy will flourish as a result of the new technologies. Jobs will be created and general prosperity would become the norm

- New technologies, e.g. in medical engineering would improve the life of the individual

- The AH system guarantees cultural integrity, meaning that the people lose nothing and keep on gaining

In the end, the individual is the big winner of the AH system. It would indeed work without the citizens, but this is not considered to be meaningful, since exclusion or even an authoritarian coercion in a model that wants to improve the lives of all is neither necessary nor expedient.

The opportunity that the AH Model actually does provoke enthusiasm among the masses and parts of the elite is a given and should also be used.

Trust and transparency

In contrast to many international institutions, all components of the AH Model must be propagated, right from the start, in terms of what they represent: a way to make the world a better place. Contrary to many other ideas, this path does not call for a radical upheaval of the individual which means that it will also enjoy a vote of confidence:

- Nation-states remain intact

- Individual systems are preserved (e.g. democratic characteristics, welfare systems)

- The market economy remains the same

- The lives of individuals are preserved
- Culture is preserved
- Identity is preserved

Changes are only necessary if there are deficiencies on the part of the state or companies that are fundamentally to the detriment of the individual.

The vote of confidence is further supported by the fact that the model also delivers sustainable technologies and provides a positive impact on companies and society in general without actually imposing changes on them.

At the same time, however, it is also necessary for the AH Fund to be accountable to parliaments and the public. Transparency is the top priority.

The end result is that the AH Model will gain support because it works and promotes good in the world. This is more than any other model has ever offered.

The idea of the AH Model as a grassroots movement

The suggestion was made in the previous section that the AH Model is capable of becoming a mass movement and it should also be considered and promoted as such:

Consider this: the AH Model is an idea that tames markets, businesses and states into voluntarily improving themselves and that always keeps what is best in mind. Such an idea will also have a reconciling effect, since many of the old conflicts will become superfluous or be simplified by the AH Model: a nationalist can support the AH Model just as much as a socialist or a liberal can. An atheist can support the model just as a religious person can. In the end, it is possible to unite all people whose personal attitude to life does not involve extremism and this is precisely something that has never before been achieved in history or at least only very, very rarely.

History also shows that far more difficult theoretical constructs with obvious deficiencies were supported with great enthusiasm. At this point it is only necessary to think of Communism, which still has many followers, but which has tended to end disastrously in its practical implementation. Likewise, reality demonstrates that states are ready to co-operate.

Why then should the AH Model fail?

Accountability and control

The AH Model contains numerous accountability and supervisory bodies:

- The participating countries determine the Supervisory Board for the Board of Directors and provide the guidelines for research and development

- The Supervisory Board determines and controls the Board of Directors

- The individual delegate of the Supervisory Board is accountable to the respective national parliament

- The AH Fund is obliged to be transparent with bi-annual reports

- The participating countries will be controlled by an independent supervisory body with regards to their behaviour and sustainability

- The companies are also carefully screened and controlled. Every collaborator is responsible for fulfilling precise transparency requirements

- Countries and enterprises are pushed towards the good by the invisible hand of nurture

Protection against abuse of power

The AH model has many control mechanisms that have already been named in the previous section. It goes without saying that corruption or abuse of power would never be ruled out 100%, but the possibility of these actions would be greatly reduced.

In principle, however, the AH Model itself is a type of misuse of power, since its market strength and market model are used to promote nurture for the better. It manipulates. And it forces. Nevertheless, it is a positive misuse of power and leads to a desirable effect: to use the egotism of the individual to achieve good for all.

Flexibility

The AH Model is flexible because it is a mechanism of flexibility. This is not only in the context of its research and development work, but also in its response to market changes. It is as dynamic as the forces of the market itself.

The AH Fund is ultimately a flexible company, not a rigid and impregnated authority.

The AH Model itself is a flexible educator that brings about change using an invisible hand.

Synopsis

The Alternative Hegemony Model is an all-encompassing approach that aims to lead the ruling conditions and orders into a new and better future. For this purpose, the AH Model makes use of existing mechanisms and guides these authorities into a more sensible direction.

The advantage of the AH Model is that it does not presuppose that humanity is "good", but that it is able to act for the good of all even if mankind only acts as a *homo economicus*. An advantage which is far more important than it appears at first sight, but which is precisely the decisive factor is that the AH Model does not oppose egotism, which would be naive. Instead, the model makes use of it. In this way it is able to defeat all forms of resistance and could offer history a profound turning point.

This turning point in history could open the gates and allow the light in, because all at once almost all of the problems which had previously appeared insurmountable and which were always addressed one at a time, will be resolvable. All that is required is the will, the confidence and the courage for the

AH Model to be implemented in but a very short time.

For, whosoever wants to make the world a better place needs a global, acceptable solution.

The Alternative Hegemony Model is such a solution by making use of nurture for the better.

Publisher

Erich von Werner Society

Understand and change –

Join us for a better world

Email:
erichvonwernersociety@understandandchange.com

www.understandandchange.com

facebook: https://www.facebook.com/Erich-von-Werner-Society-Understand-and-change-353251871900615

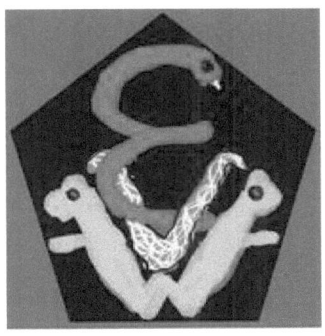

Author

Andreas Herteux

Andreas Herteux is a german philosopher, author and economist.

www.andreasherteux.com
www.facebook.com/andreasherteux

Publisher

Erich von Werner Verlag

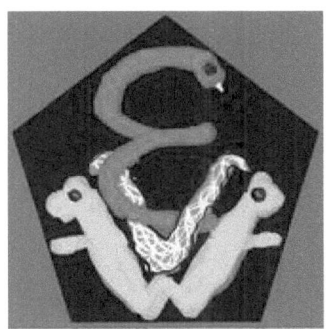

www.erichvonwernerverlag.de
www.facebook.com/erichvonwernerverlag
www.twitter.com/ErichvonWerner

Email: info@erichvonwernerverlag.de

Birkenfelder Straße 3

97842 Karbach

GERMANY